Can I really trust the Bible?

And other questions about Scripture,
truth, and how God speaks

Barry Cooper

Questions
Christians ask

Can I really trust the Bible?
And other questions about Scripture, truth, and how God speaks
© Barry Cooper/The Good Book Company, 2014
Reprinted 2015

Published by
The Good Book Company
Tel (UK): 0333 123 0880
Tel (North America): (1) 866 244 2165
International: +44 (0) 208 942 0880
Email (UK): info@thegoodbook.co.uk
Email (North America): info@thegoodbook.com

Websites
UK & Europe: www.thegoodbook.co.uk
North America: www.thegoodbook.com
Australia: www.thegoodbook.com.au
New Zealand: www.thegoodbook.co.nz

ISBN: 9781909559134

Printed in the UK by CPI Group (UK) Ltd, Croydon, CR0 4YY
Design by André Parker

Contents

For Graham Cooper

Introduction

"The Bible is full of wonderful stories. Like, amazing stories. And there's lots of wisdom in it. But some of it is very weird... And most of it is very outdated."

New Delhi, India, 1991. As he spoke, he smiled at me in a patient, good-natured way, the way someone might smile at a two-year-old trying to access voicemail on an iPhone.

"Then there are the miracles, which you have to take with a *B-I-G* pinch of salt. Plus obviously it's been corrupted over time as it's been passed on. So I just think people should take what's helpful, and not get so hung up on it."

When the conversation began, I would've described myself as a Christian. Midway through, I was reeling. Now that it was over, I knew I wasn't a Christian at all.

Here was one of the most intelligent, likeable people I'd ever met. And he'd reached the conclusion that intelligent, likeable people just did not trust the Bible.

At breakfast the next morning, I was told there'd been an earthquake during the night. Apparently, I'd slept right through it. But those questions ... I was still shaking from those questions. *Can you really trust the Bible? Can you be absolutely sure of this book you're building your life on? Can you know for certain that it actually is God's word? How can you know?*

Perhaps you remember Winnie-the-Pooh, the honey-obsessed bear who lived in Ashdown Forest. He faced a similar question. Here he is, staring at a jar, and wondering if he can be sure of what's inside:

It had HUNNY written on it, but, just to make sure, he took off the paper cover and looked at it, and it looked just like honey. "But you never can tell," said Pooh. "I remember my uncle saying once that he had seen cheese just this colour." So he put his tongue in, and took a large lick. "Yes," he said, "it is. No doubt about that."

Pooh may have been a simple bear in profound danger of early-onset diabetes, but what if we were to approach the Bible in the same way he approached the honey? Like this:

1. Does the Bible *claim to be* God's word? What does it say on the outside of the jar? Does the Bible have anything to say about itself?

2. Does the Bible *seem to be* God's word? What does it look like when we "take off the cover" and peer inside? Does the Bible look like something only God could have written?

3. Does the Bible *prove to be* God's word? What does it taste like? Can we know, in our own personal experience, that the Bible really is God's word?

Over the next five chapters, I'll try to answer those three questions. Whether you're a Christian or not, I pray it'll be helpful. And if by any chance you're the young man from New Delhi: thank you, my friend. I hope we meet again.

Chapter 1

Does the Bible claim to be God's word?

The world, the word, and what Jesus thought of the Bible

Imagine a sun-bleached, tropical shore. We're standing there, enjoying the view. Suddenly, a man in a tuxedo staggers out of the surf and stops in front of us.

"Where do you think he's come from?" I ask.

"No idea", you reply.

"Maybe he's a holidaymaker who's fallen off a cruise liner", I suggest.

"Maybe he's like, a really well-dressed pirate?" you also suggest. (We both laugh at this point.)

"Huh", we both shrug. "Guess we'll never know."

And off we both go, leaving tuxedo man dripping onto the sand.

Was it odd that it never occurred to either of us to ask the man himself where he was from? He might lie, of course. But if he's standing there right in front of us, ready to speak, wouldn't it be rude—and even a little foolish—to ignore what he has to say?

So in that spirit, before we start guessing what the Bible is and where it's come from, let's ask the Bible itself: *What do you claim to be?*

What does the Old Testament claim to be?

Open a Bible about halfway through.

You should find yourself in the middle of a collection of songs called "Psalms". Psalm 19 describes two ways in which God speaks to us: firstly through his world, and secondly through his word.

First of all, the world:

> The heavens declare the glory of God;
>> the skies proclaim the work of his hands.
> Day after day they pour forth speech;
>> night after night they reveal knowledge.
> They have no speech, they use no words;
>> no sound is heard from them.
> Yet their voice goes out into all the earth,
>> their words to the ends of the world.
>
> *Psalm 19 v 1-4*[1]

The writer is telling us that God "speaks" to the world, through the world. The beautiful things he has made "declare" his glory—his greatness, his kindness, his cre-

---

1   All Bible quotations are from the New International Version unless otherwise noted. (Why so many versions? More on this later.) If you're unfamiliar with Bible references, the number before the "v" is the chapter, and the number after is the verse. So "Psalm 19 v 1-4" means the book of Psalms, chapter 19, verses 1 to 4.

ativity, his provision for each one of us. The grandeur of the sky and the stars have a way of drawing our eyes upwards, towards something—or someone—beyond them. Mute as they are, they are communicating something to "all the earth ... to the ends of the world". By the fact of their existence, they constantly sing: *There is a Maker! He is powerful and beautiful and good. He created you, just as he created us. He sustains you—day after day— just as he sustains us.*

Look at the next two verses. Notice that the sun also tells us about God:

> In the heavens God has pitched a tent for the sun.
>> It is like a bridegroom coming out of his chamber,
>> like a champion rejoicing to run his course.
> It rises at one end of the heavens
>> and makes its circuit to the other;
>> nothing is deprived of its warmth.
>
> *Psalm 19 v 5-6*

The sun rising is "like a bridegroom coming out of his chamber", like a man emerging from his bedroom the morning after his wedding night. He's having trouble suppressing the enormous smile on his face. He is filled with joy, he is glowing, he is radiating warmth. This, too, communicates something about God's life-giving goodness. Every time the sun rises, and "makes its circuit" across the sky—like a triumphant athlete enjoying a lap of honour—it is sharing with us the joy, the generosity, the warmth of our Creator. I am like this, the sun seems to say, because my Creator is like this.

Just as a painting reveals the qualities of a painter, God's world speaks powerfully of him. Even if we were to burn all the Bibles, and drown all the preachers, the psalmist says that God would still make his beauty known through the skies, the stars and the sun. And this, incidentally, is why the Bible doesn't try to prove the existence of a Creator. It's just assumed to be as unmissable as the colossal flaming globe hanging over our heads.

The world is not enough

But there's only so much a star can say. A painting may be wonderful, but what it tells me about the artist is limited. I'd need to read her autobiography to get to know what she's really like.

At the risk of over-simplifying, that is what the Bible claims to be: God's autobiography. It is the way we get to know him. The world doesn't tell us enough. We need the word.

Now, that's not to say the Bible contains everything there is to know about God. Not even close. But it does claim to reveal all we *need* to know about our Creator, and all we need to know in order to live lives pleasing to him. This is what theologians call the "sufficiency" of Scripture. One Bible writer puts it like this:

the Holy Scriptures ... are able to make you
wise for salvation through faith in Christ Jesus.
All Scripture is God-breathed and is useful for

teaching, rebuking, correcting and training in righteousness, so that the servant of God may be *thoroughly* equipped for every good work.

2 Timothy 3 v 15-17[1]

The Bible gives us what we need to know if we're to experience the highest, deepest, widest, most satisfying joy in life: God himself.

That's why, in the next few verses of Psalm 19, our focus moves from the world to the word:

The law of the LORD [God's word] is perfect,
      refreshing the soul.
The statutes of the LORD are trustworthy,
      making wise the simple.
The precepts of the LORD are right,
      giving joy to the heart.
The commands of the LORD are radiant,
      giving light to the eyes.
The fear of the LORD is pure,
      enduring forever.
The decrees of the LORD are firm,
      and all of them are righteous.
They are more precious than gold,
      than much pure gold;
they are sweeter than honey,
      than honey from the honeycomb.

Psalm 19 v 7-10

Did you see it? Again and again, the writer draws atten-

---

1   My emphasis. From now on, all *italics* in Bible quotations are my own.

tion to the fact that the Scriptures are from God. They're not just laws or statutes or precepts or commands or decrees; they're "the law *of the* LORD ... the statutes *of the* LORD ... the precepts *of the* LORD ... the commands *of the* LORD ... the decrees *of the* LORD". The claim of Psalm 19 is that the Old Testament was created by God, just as surely as he created the world.

Dig deeper into the Bible, and you'll find that it closely connects the life-giving power of God's spoken word with the life-giving power of his written word. For example, Genesis 1 describes every atom of the universe, including humanity itself, being created and ordered with symphonic precision by God's *spoken* words. Each new act of creation is preceded by the significant phrase: "And God *said*...", just to make it clear that it is God's *word* that brings everything into being.

Then, just as God's *spoken* word brought light into being in Genesis 1 v 3, so, as we've just seen in Psalm 19, his *written* word is described as "giving light to the eyes". As the psalm implies, God's written word is no less powerful or life-giving than his spoken word. If this is true, then when we read God's word, or hear it preached, we should read or listen with trembling and anticipation. The fierce power that summoned and sustains the universe is about to be unleashed again in our hearing.

Theologian Francis Schaeffer sums it up: the Old Testament sees itself as "the written record of the words of God as they were given by God, and as they were recorded by men who were specially designated and commanded by God to this work." This written record "was preserved by the Jewish people and accepted by them as authoritative." The New Testament writers agree. For example, the Apostle Paul describes the Old Testament as "the very words of God" (Romans 3 v 2). "Apostle", by the way, means one of those who had been a personal eyewitness of Jesus' resurrection, and had been specifically commissioned and empowered by Christ to tell others what they had seen.

In fact, in the first five books of the Old Testament alone, you'll see phrases like "God said" about 700 times. There are nearly 4,000 such claims in the Old Testament as a whole. At the very least, then, both Old and New Testaments claim that the Old Testament is "the word of God".

And that's the way Jesus saw it too.

Jesus' claims about the Old Testament

Jessica is 24, well educated, and a Christian. She doesn't read her Bible that much, but then life is "pretty busy". She's excited, she says, about being a follower of Christ, but is much less excited about reading a book written thousands of years ago and thousands of miles away.

Jesus is 30. He is the uneducated son of a wood-worker, born in a hick town in first century Palestine. He also claims to be the eternal Son of God, the second person of the Trinity, and the promised Messiah who has come from God to rescue his people from slavery to sin, Satan and death. Everywhere he goes, he is besieged by crowds who hang on his words, and cry out to be healed. He, too, is pretty busy. But unlike Jessica, he is completely captivated by God's word.

You can hear it in the way he speaks: "It is written...
it is written... it is written..." Over and over again, he
appeals to God's written word. He trusts it implicitly. In
Jesus' mind, there is no higher authority than the written word of God. Extraordinary really, that a person of
his evident power would lean so heavily on a *book*.

Just listen to the way he talks about the Old Testament.

> Everything *must* be fulfilled that is written about
> me in the Law of Moses, the Prophets and the
> Psalms.   *Luke 24 v 44*

"The Law of Moses, the Prophets and the Psalms" was a
common way of describing the Old Testament. According to Jesus, then, everything written about him in the
Old Testament *must* happen. Why? Because, according
to Jesus, it is written in Scripture, and everything written there is completely trustworthy because it comes
from God. Jesus reiterates his point when he says simply: "Scripture cannot be broken" (John 10 v 35, ESV).

But Jesus didn't just talk about the authority of the
Bible. He showed it in the way he lived—and died.

When tempted, Jesus *appealed* to it. Matthew records
three temptations (Matthew 4 v 1-10), and on each occasion, Jesus responds with quotations from the Old
Testament preceded by the words: "It is written...".

When his religious opponents tried to catch him
out, Jesus *rested* on it. He knew that they too trusted the
divine authority of Scripture. He told them the reason
their teaching was wrong was because they didn't know

their Bibles properly: "You are in error because you do not know the Scriptures or the power of God" (Matthew 22 v 29). Far from being *full* of errors, Jesus insisted that the Scriptures are necessary if we're to keep ourselves *from* error. (This, by the way, is what theologians call the "necessity" of Scripture.)

When he was experiencing the most unrelenting, excruciating pain, he *quoted* it: "My God, my God, why have you forsaken me?" (see Psalm 22 v 1).

When he spoke to the crowds, Jesus *upheld* it:

> Do not think that I have come to abolish the Law or the Prophets [ie: the commands and promises of the Old Testament]; I have not come to abolish them but to fulfil them. For truly, I tell you, until heaven and earth disappear, not the smallest letter, nor the least stroke of a pen, will by any means disappear from the Law until everything is accomplished.   *Matthew 5 v 17-18*

According to Jesus, then, even the tiniest fleck of Old Testament punctuation has divine weight and authority.

One of the most stunning illustrations of this comes in Matthew 19 v 4-6. "Haven't you read," says Jesus, "that at the beginning the Creator 'made them male and female' and said, 'For this reason a man will leave his father and mother and be united to his wife, and the two will become one flesh.'" Jesus is here quoting Genesis 2 v 24, clearly believing it to be the word of God himself. But turn back to that verse and you'll notice that it's not God speaking—it's the narrator of Genesis.

Jesus, in other words, does not distinguish between the words of God, and the words of the biblical writer. If the narrator of Genesis reports something, for Jesus it is as if God himself has spoken.

Similarly, he makes no bones about the historical truthfulness of the Old Testament. Adam and Eve, Cain and Abel, Noah, Abraham, Isaac, Jacob, Jonah, Elisha, Elijah, Moses, Daniel, David, Solomon and Isaiah—all are referenced by Jesus as real, flesh-and-blood human beings.

If we doubt the authority of the Old Testament, or we'd rather cut out some of the things we read in it, all this puts us in a difficult position. To say that we cannot really trust it is to claim—at a distance of a few thousand years—that we (or the scholars we've put our trust in) can see straighter than the Jewish religious authorities, the Jewish people, the writers of the New Testament, and Jesus Christ himself.

What's inside the Bible?

The Bible is divided into two sections: the Old Testament (39 documents, written in Hebrew with a smattering of Aramaic) and the New Testament (27 documents, written in Greek, again with an occasional dash of Aramaic). The documents in the Old Testament were all written before Jesus Christ was born, with the oldest being written about 1500 years BC. The ones in the New Testament were all written after he was born, with the latest being written in about AD 90, roughly 60 years after Jesus' crucifixion.

Incidentally, the word "testament" is another word for "covenant", a binding contract or agreement. So what we have in our Bibles is the documentary evidence of two agreements—Old and New—between God and his people. Both are complementary, with each part shedding light on the other, rather like two halves of a sentence. These two "testaments" reveal God's purpose in human history: to redeem a people who will glorify him by enjoying him for ever.

Chances are your Bible is divided into chapters and verses. But these divisions weren't a feature of the earliest documents. They were added later to help readers find their way around. The chapter numbers were inserted by Stephen Langton, Archbishop of Canterbury early in the 13th century. The Old Testament verse numbers were added by Jewish scribes around 900 AD, and the New Testament verse numbers by a French printer called Robert Estienne in the 16th century.

What does the New Testament claim to be?

The New Testament writings claim to be as authoritative as the Old Testament.

The Apostle Paul wrote around half of the documents in the New Testament. He said this: "If anyone thinks they are a prophet or otherwise gifted by the Spirit, let them acknowledge that *what I am writing to you is the Lord's command*" (1 Corinthians 14 v 37). He commended those who accepted his message, because they "accepted it not as a human word, but *as it actually is, the word of God*" (1 Thessalonians 2 v 13).

Peter, another New Testament writer and Apostle

who hadn't always seen eye-to-eye with Paul (see Galatians 2 v 11), strongly confirmed Paul's claim:

> His letters contain some things that are hard to understand, which ignorant and unstable people distort, as they do the other Scriptures, to their own destruction.   *2 Peter 3 v 16*

Fascinating! Notice how Peter comments—in passing, as if it were a common assumption—that Paul's letters are on a par with "the *other* Scriptures". For him, Paul's writing had as much claim to be "God's word" as the Old Testament. Peter made similar claims for himself, saying that his teaching was enabled "by the Holy Spirit sent from heaven"(1 Peter 1 v 12).

Likewise, the Apostle John. He begins his writing at one point by claiming that the resurrected Christ has given him the vision he's about to describe, instructing him to "write on a scroll what you see...", John announces plainly that what he has written is "the word of God and the testimony of Jesus Christ" (Revelation 1 v 2, 11-19).

How could Paul, Peter and John make such bold, and potentially even blasphemous claims?

Jesus and the New Testament

The answer comes in John's Gospel. Here, Jesus makes a series of remarkable promises to the Apostles—those who would personally write the majority of the New Testament. (The remainder of the New Testament documents were authored either by those writing under the direction of an Apostle, or by those who were eyewitnesses and companions of Jesus.)

First, he promises the Apostles that when he leaves them, the Holy Spirit will remind them of his words:

> The Holy Spirit, whom the Father will send in my name, will teach you all things and will remind you of everything I have said to you.
>
> *John 14 v 26*

Then, Jesus repeats the promise that the Holy Spirit will enable them to write truthfully about him. He also adds the command that they, as Apostles, must tell the world about the events they have personally witnessed:

> When the Advocate comes, whom I will send to you from the Father—the Spirit of truth who goes out from the Father—he will testify about me. And you also must testify, for you have been with me from the beginning. *John 15 v 26-27*

Shortly afterwards, Jesus again promises that the Apostles will be guided "into all truth" by the Holy Spirit. Not only will they remember truthfully what has happened, but they will also be told truthfully what will happen in the future:

> But when he, the Spirit of truth, comes, he will guide you into all the truth. He will not speak on his own; he will speak only what he hears, and he will tell you what is yet to come. *John 16 v 13*

So Jesus himself promised the Apostles that they would accurately preserve his words and teaching for us. He commanded them to do it, and then empowered them to do it by his own Spirit.

But doesn't this argument just go round in circles?

When I say: "The Bible says that the Bible is trustworthy", someone might object: "That's a circular argument".

"Ok," I say, "what do you think?"

"Well," they begin, "from a rational point of view..."

"Wait, why should we see things 'from a rational point of view'?"

"Well, because it's rational."

And at that point, my friend reveals her own circularity. In a sense, she is opening up her own bible—one marked "rationalism". She's saying we should believe rationalism because rationalism says it's true. And for "rationalism" you can substitute "materialism" or "Islam" or "Mormonism" or "atheism" (or whatever), depending on which way you're inclined.

When you think about it, it's impossible for any of us to avoid this kind of circularity in our arguments: we all appeal to authority of one kind or another, even when we don't realise it.

Secondly, if I say: "The Bible is my highest authority because it can be proved rationally", the argument would be self-defeating. I'd be appealing to an authority other than the Bible (rationalism), implying that it (and not God's word) was the real measure of trustworthiness.

That's why it's good to hear the claims the Bible makes about itself. We shouldn't reject them simply because the Bible makes them. In fact, if the Bible really is what it claims, it must be—to use an impressive-sounding phrase—self-authenticating. To borrow the line of Hilary of Poitiers, the 4th-century theologian: "Only God is a fit witness to himself".

Chapter 2

Does the Bible claim to be God's word?

The word, the Word
and the rightness of writing

The word or the Word? The Bible describes God's written or spoken self-expression as "the word of God". But the Bible also speaks of the (capital W) "Word of God".

Look at the way John's Gospel begins:

> In the beginning was the Word, and the Word was with God, and the Word was God. He was with God in the beginning. Through him all things were made; without him nothing was made that has been made ... The Word became flesh and made his dwelling among us. We have seen his glory, the glory of the one and only Son, who came from the Father, full of grace and truth. *John 1 v 1-3, 14*

Here, John is describing Jesus Christ as "the Word". Apparently, God's word is not just an "it", it's also a "he". How so?

You and I reveal ourselves through our words. Words disclose our thoughts, our intentions, our character. We're like this because the One who created us is like this (Genesis 1 v 27). He, too, reveals himself with words. But most of all, he reveals himself with "*the* Word", Jesus Christ.

The writer of Hebrews puts it this way:

> In the past God spoke to our ancestors through the prophets at many times and in various ways, but in these last days he has spoken to us by his Son, whom he appointed heir of all things, and through whom also he made the universe. The Son is the radiance of God's glory and the exact representation of his being, sustaining all things by his powerful word.   *Hebrews 1 v 1-3*

Notice that stunning phrase: Jesus is "the exact representation" of God's being. As another Bible writer puts it: "God was pleased to have all his fullness dwell in him" (Colossians 1 v 19). Jesus himself says the same: "Whatever the Father does the Son also does" (John 5 v 19).

That's why Jesus is described as the (capital W) Word. He is *the Word* because he is the definitive revealing of who God is and what God is like. When we look at Jesus—all that he said and did—most of the guessing games about God tail off into silence.

"It's not about knowing a book..."

Just to be clear, God is not two-faced. He doesn't say one thing in the Bible and then another thing in Jesus. The two are inseparably connected. God makes himself known through Jesus, who is revealed in the Bible.

As we saw in the last chapter, Jesus repeatedly points to Scripture: the Word points to the word. At the same time, Scripture points to Jesus: the word points to the Word.

Jesus himself is explicit about this when he says, "These are the very Scriptures that testify about me" (John 5 v 39). That's why he lambasts the Bible scholars of his day: they spend their lives studying the Scriptures, but they won't allow the Scriptures to lead them to the person the Scriptures speak of. They want the word, but they do not want the Word.

In our day, religious or "spiritual" people frequently make the reverse mistake. We want the Word, but we do not want the word. I once appeared on a Christian television show where the host said: "And remember, being a Christian is not about knowing a book. It's about knowing a person." The reality is that we cannot have the latter without the former. We can't know Jesus apart from the Bible because, as Jesus himself says, the Bible always and on every page testifies to him. Any other "Jesus" is just a Jesus of our own imagining.

Fully human and fully divine

There's another connection between "the word" and "the Word". Both are fully human, yet fully divine.

The word (the Bible) never denies its humanity. It was written down by human beings, each with their own distinct personalities, experiences and ways of writing. As a result, it speaks to us where we are. There was no unfeeling, robotic dictation, with the human writer used merely as a secretary. The humanity of God's word is evident on every page. At the same time, the Holy Spirit worked in each writer to ensure that the words being written down were fully truthful.

Similarly, the Word (Jesus) never denied his humanity. In Jesus, God reveals himself to be one who understands and sympathises with our frailties and temptations. At the same time, Jesus was clear that his humanity took nothing away from his divinity: "I and the Father are one" (John 10 v 30). If we're followers of Christ, we have little difficulty accepting that *the Word* was fully human yet fully divine. We should approach *the word* in the same way.

Why did God communicate in writing?

Isn't it silly to claim that something as commonplace as a book actually contains God's words? If God really is God, couldn't he communicate with human beings in a less run-of-the-mill way?

He certainly could. The Bible itself gives plenty of examples: God speaks to people by means of dreams, visions, angels—even, on one significant occasion, from a burning bush. He also "speaks" to individuals by means of their consciences (Romans 2 v 15); by hard-wiring us with a deep inner hunger for him (Ecclesiastes 3 v 11); even by determining where and when in history we live (Acts 17 v 26-27). God constantly "speaks" to us of his goodness by providing for us, regardless of whether we love him or not (Matthew 5 v 45; Acts 14 v 17). And he still guides his people by means of his Holy Spirit.

But if we were to hear a voice speaking directly to us, a voice claiming to be God himself, how would we know it was God speaking and not just indigestion, our own desires, or something worse? And what if we just "feel" that something is right? Would that be God guiding us?

The Apostle John addresses this in 1 John 4 verse 1: "Dear friends, do not believe every spirit, but test the spirits to see whether they are from God, because many false prophets have gone out into the world". The way we "test the spirits" is to measure everything against God's written word. If any voice chafes against Scripture at any point, then according to Scripture it shouldn't be treated as being "from God".

That is one of the reasons why God has chosen to communicate in writing. It gives us a supreme court in which to weigh up every human claim to be speaking or acting with God's authority. And this is a very good thing. If every person claimed to have heard words from God, and acted on them apart from any other consideration, the result would be chaos. As the 17th-century theologian John Owen put it, the "mask of pretended revelations and interior inspiration" has been used by Satan to mislead people throughout history. It's a loving gesture of God's grace, then, that he has provided Scripture as "a constant aid and guide".[1]

---

1 John Owen, *Biblical Theology* (Grand Rapids: Soli Deo Gloria Publications, 2007), 829-32.

Write this down

There's another reason God has communicated in writing. Writing was the natural way to preserve God's words for present and future generations.[1]

For example, the Ten Commandments are described as having been "inscribed by the finger of God" (Exodus 31 v 18), and when the stone tablets were smashed by Moses—in a fit of anger at Israel's idolatry—God immediately took steps to replace them. Writing was the way God carefully protected his words so that they would not be lost, changed, distorted or forgotten. As he says to Moses at one point: "Write this on a scroll as something to be remembered..." (Exodus 17 v 14).

Similarly, there's a wonderful moment in Psalm 102 where the psalmist says: "Let this be *written* for a future generation, that a people not yet created may praise the Lord" (Psalm 102 v 18). I hope you can feel the wonder of that. If you're a follower of Jesus, or you're soon to become one, you are one of those he mentions here as "a people not yet created". The psalmist, writing about 2,500 years ago, was self-consciously writing down God's words with you in mind.

Again, in the Bible's final book, we read:

> He who was seated on the throne said, "I am making everything new!" Then he said, "*Write this down*, for these words are trustworthy and true." *Revelation 21 v 5*

---

1   See Exodus 24 v 4; 34 v 27; Numbers 33:2; Deuteronomy 31 v 9; Job 19 v 23; Isaiah 30 v 8; Jeremiah 36 v 2; 45 v 1; 51 v 60.

So there's no reason to be suspicious of the Bible's divine authority simply because it's a book. Words don't become less authoritative because they're written rather than spoken.

In fact, when you think about it, the reverse is true. The most important statements human beings make—whether they be legally-binding contracts or lyrical expressions of love—are most often written down, at least when we intend them to be powerful and lasting. When God specifically instructs that his words be written down, things get serious.

Why the words in the Bible matter

God ensured that his words were preserved in writing because they are a matter of life and death. Eternal life and eternal death.

At one point in Jesus' life, many of his disciples turned back and no longer followed him. Looking at the twelve disciples who were closest to him, he asked: "You do not want to leave too, do you?" And Peter, so often the spokesman for the group, said this:

> Lord, to whom shall we go? *You have the words of eternal life*. We have come to believe and to know that you are the Holy One of God.
>
> *John 6 v 68-69*

Jesus has the words of eternal life. Now, that's wonderful for those living in Palestine 2,000 years ago—those who could listen to him speaking in the flesh—but what about us? How can we know what his words were? Is eternal life eternally lost to us because we were born too late to hear them?

Thank God that isn't the case. These "words of eternal life" have been preserved for us. Without those words, we would still be unreconciled with God the Father, with nothing to look forward to except death, judgment and hell. Without those words, we would never have known about God the Son, who died, was resurrected, and then ascended so that we could become a child of God, a co-heir with Christ. Without those words, we would never have known about God the Holy Spirit, who graciously comes to live in those who belong to him.

So when people who claim to be Christian are careless with (or selectively trash) the very words which brought them life, it is tragic—and absurd. Imagine a person drowning in the Atlantic who, having been rescued by a passing life-raft, proceeds to pick holes in it.

As Peter said, Jesus has the words of eternal life. There is no one else who has them. Without a record of them, we are lost. The Bible itself is explicit about this:

> Jesus performed many other signs in the presence of his disciples, which are not recorded in this book. *But these are written that you may believe that Jesus is the Messiah, the Son of God, and that by believing you may have life in his name.*
> *John 20 v 30-31*

God has preserved his word in the Bible so that we ourselves might be preserved. He wants us to have life, as we meet the source of all life—Jesus himself—in Scripture.

Isn't the Bible socially, culturally and sexually out of date? Isn't it just a product of its time?

The past often embarrasses us. Looking at photos of myself growing up in the 1980s, it's one fashion car-crash after another. It's impossible to look away. Why didn't people spend the entire decade pointing at each other and laughing? The reason, I suppose, is that more or less everyone was dressed the same. It seemed normal to us. We'd built up a plausibility structure of pastel t-shirts, neon socks and snow-washed jeans.

Isn't it the same when we look at the Bible? It reflects the attitudes of a particular time and place in history. It seemed ok to everyone at the time, but now those attitudes appear regressive and embarrassing. We look back and we say to ourselves: *"What were they thinking? I'm glad we know better"*.

But then, a troubling thought occurs. How can we be *sure* we know better? What will we think of what we're wearing now, in 20 years' time? Right now, a bearded man in heavy-rimmed specs, skinny jeans and a flannel shirt seems very plausible—especially if we're living in the west, in a large urban centre, and working in media or design. But will we look back one day and say: *"What were we thinking"*?

Many social, cultural and sexual views which seem self-evidently right to most people currently living in London or Manhattan did not seem right to Londoners and Manhattanites 200 years ago. And they don't seem right to most people currently living in Nairobi or Jakarta. Presumably, we'll believe something else in 200 years' time. If we dismiss biblical teaching as being a product of its time and place, we have to be honest and recognise that we ourselves—the ones offering the criticism—are just as much a product of ours.

And incidentally, the first disciples didn't think Jesus' teaching was a product of its time. Many of them were so shocked by how counter-cultural it was, they packed up and left (John 6 v 60-66). Nor did Jesus' teaching seem uncontroversial to the political leaders, the religious authorities, or the general public. His words and actions resulted in him being mocked, tortured, stripped naked, and nailed to a cross.

If we feel discomfort at some of the Bible's teaching, is it really because the Bible is a product of its time, or because we are?

And there's something else that's worth considering. We may find ourselves rejecting God's word (or parts of it) because it expresses views different to our own. But isn't it comically small-minded and arrogant to assume that God, if he's there, would always agree with us? If God really is God, and the Bible is his word, wouldn't we expect him occasionally to contradict and correct us? Wouldn't it be suspicious if he always said what we wanted him to say, or if he always confirmed the views of our particular culture, in our particular moment of history?

We should expect Scripture, if it is what it claims to be, to challenge all of us at some point or other. And that's what we find as we read it. Throughout history, and across cultures, the Bible has been an equal-opportunity offender of all people, everywhere—even when it was first written.

Hasn't the Bible been used to justify terrible things?

There's no doubt that the Bible has been used to justify violence, slavery, and oppression.[1] For many, that's ample enough reason to reject it. How can we say that it's the word of God when it has been wielded in such dreadful ways?

At first glance, this seems like a legitimate response. But it's also true that the Bible has been used to *oppose* violence, slavery and oppression. Famously, for example, the reformer William Wilberforce (who led the movement to abolish the slave trade in the late 18th/early 19th century) was driven by his evangelical Christian beliefs. Or take Martin Luther King's campaigning for civil rights and racial equality. Or think of Corrie ten Boom, the Dutch Christian who risked her life to help Jews escape the Nazi holocaust during the Second World War.

---

1   The currently popular idea that religion is the main cause of war and oppression doesn't stand up, however. "In terms of casualties, religious wars account for only 2% of all people killed by warfare. This pales in comparison to the number of people who have been killed by secular dictators in the 20th century alone." See "Devastating Arguments Against Christianity", http://wellspentjourney. wordpress.com/2013/10/01/devastating-arguments-against-christianity-courtesy-of-the-internet/ (accessed 30th January, 2014).

It would be unwise of us to despise carving knives because people sometimes fail to use them as the designer intended. In fact, the very feature that makes a carving knife so wonderfully effective in the right hands—its sharpness—is the very reason it can be so terribly damaging in the wrong hands. Men and women have sometimes taken the sharpness of God's word and used it unwisely, or even wickedly. For that, it would be foolish to blame the Bible.

As the old saying goes: *"The same sun that melts wax, hardens clay"*—but no one gets angry at the sun.

Conclusion

So far we've seen that both the Old and New Testaments *claim to be* documents with unique and divine authority, preserved for the eternal good of future generations.

But what does the Bible *seem to be* when we open it up and look inside? Does it look like honey?

Chapter 3

Does the Bible seem to be God's word?

Consistency, conspiracies and corruptions

Imagine a radio with 66 stations. As you flick rapidly between them, you notice something very odd. The songs sound different—country and western collides with hip hop collides with opera—but each new vocalist is developing the same story.

The Bible contains 66 documents.[1] Approximately 40 authors wrote in three different languages over a period of about 1,500 years. Some of the authors were young, some were old; some were professionals, others were peasants; some were soldiers, others were civil servants, fishermen, farmers, or kings. They wrote in wildly different genres: history, population statistics, poetry, travel diaries, law, prophecy, family trees, biography, geographical surveys, architectural blueprints, song lyrics. They wrote in dif-

---

1 Some traditions, such as Roman Catholicism, add extra documents. More on that in a moment.

ferent periods of history, in different geographical locations, to different groups of people. It wasn't like a relay race, with one author handing on the baton to another. Often, the authors wrote centuries apart.

Consider that for a moment. What if multiple authors had each written a single page of this little book you're holding? What if each author wrote in different genres, in different centuries and in different countries, with no "master plan" for them to consult? What is the likelihood that it would make any sense at all?

Yet the Bible has a single theme running all the way through it, like rings in the trunk of a tree. It tells the unified, coherent story of humanity's creation by God, humanity's rebellion against God, and God's redemption of his people. It's like flicking between 66 different stations and finding that each is advancing the same story, a grand symphonic drama that grows in beauty as it develops.

As well as having a single theme, the Bible has a single hero. Each of these 66 documents, even the ones written hundreds of years before Jesus' birth, are all singing the same song. And the song, consistently, is about Jesus. As Jesus said: "These are the very Scriptures that testify about *me*" (John 5 v 39).

What are the odds?

2 Peter chapter 1 offers an explanation for this stunning single-mindedness.

1. The writers weren't part of a conspiracy

You'll find 2 Peter chapter 1 near the end of your Bible. It was written by the Apostle Peter, who was one of

Jesus' closest followers during the three years of Jesus' public ministry. Let's start reading at verse 16:

> For we did not follow cleverly devised stories
> when we told you about the coming of our Lord
> Jesus Christ in power. *2 Peter 1 v 16*

Peter is very clear: neither he, nor the other New Testament writers, were dreaming up a new religious myth when they wrote what they did. They weren't part of some pan-mediterranean conspiracy. They just don't fit the profile of people trying to "follow cleverly devised stories": they had nothing to gain in terms of money or protection or worldly power. In fact, the reverse was true. They had everything to lose, and they knew it. Peter was imprisoned repeatedly, and was eventually executed for continuing to speak and write as he did. (Origen, a theologian writing in about AD 230, reports that Peter was eventually crucified upside-down.)

So why did Peter continue to talk about Jesus?

2. The writers were eyewitnesses

When you witness something remarkable, it's hard to keep quiet about it. Peter wrote because he—and most of the New Testament writers[1]—were "eyewitnesses of [Jesus'] majesty". After what they'd seen, it was impossible *not* to speak:

---

1   Not all the New Testament writers were personal eyewitnesses. Some (eg: Mark and Luke) were *guided* by personal eyewitnesses as they wrote. For example, it's widely accepted that the Apostle Peter oversaw the writing of Mark's Gospel.

He received honour and glory from God the
Father when the voice came to him from the Ma-
jestic Glory, saying, "This is my Son, whom I love;
with him I am well pleased." *We ourselves* heard
this voice that came from heaven when we were
with him.   *2 Peter 1 v 16-18*

When Peter writes: "*We ourselves* heard this voice that
came from heaven", he's driving home the point that this
isn't second-hand information. He's reporting his own experience. And not just his experience, either. There was
more than one witness, as the "we" makes clear.[1]

What becomes very clear as we read the New Testament is that the Bible documents aren't the wild-eyed
delusions of lone religious fruitcakes who've spent way
too much time in a cave. Many of the remarkable events
described in the Bible are historical incidents which
had multiple eyewitnesses; hundreds, even thousands
of eyewitnesses. The ancient historian Luke (who authored one of the four biographies of Jesus at the start
of the New Testament) wrote that he had "carefully in-
vestigated everything from the beginning". Central to
that investigation was eyewitness testimony. He writes:

Many have undertaken to draw up an account of
the things that have been fulfilled among us, just
as they were handed down to us by those who
from the first were eyewitnesses.   *Luke 1 v 1-3*

To give another example, when Paul writes about the

---

1   Matthew 17 v 1 tells us that he's talking about himself, James and John.

resurrection of Jesus, he's not asking his readers to accept something that only a handful of people claim to have seen. The same Jesus who was killed publicly was then seen alive publicly—by hundreds of witnesses. On one occasion, more than 500 people saw Jesus alive and well *at the same time*, just a few days after his public execution. Most of those people were still alive when the New Testament documents were originally circulated, so that if the claim of Jesus' resurrection was fabricated, it could easily have been shot down (1 Corinthians 15 v 3-6). In fact, it was in the best interests of the Roman Empire and the Jewish authorities to discredit these ideas, because they represented a clear and present danger to their own authority.

But tellingly, they couldn't. These things happened in public. And the certainty of physical resurrection—a reality that Peter had personally verified, having physically interacted with the risen Jesus—helps to explain why his own death no longer held any fear for him.

Isn't reported/oral information unreliable?

Some Bible writers weren't personal eyewitnesses of the events they describe. They depended on the spoken testimony of others. Does that necessarily mean their writing is less reliable?

This is an assumption that many people make, including my friend in New Delhi. "It's based on oral tradition," they say, "therefore it almost certainly didn't happen, or the information has been hopelessly corrupted."

But is that necessarily the case? I know I was born on November 4th, but only because someone told me. The information was handed down to me, orally. I don't remember the birth myself (though apparently I was present), and my birth certificate could very easily have been forged. So when I tell you I was born on November 4th, it is a statement based on reported information and trust. Still, I'm confident the statement is true, and people have been willing to trust me on it.

All that to say: orally transmitted information isn't necessarily unreliable, any more than written documents are necessarily reliable.

How can I trust the Bible when it has miracles in it?

The presence of the supernatural in the Bible can be problematic for some.

However, if God *does* exist—and the eyewitness accounts of Jesus' life give us very good reason for believing so—then the temporary suspension of natural laws would be consistent with that fact. How else could God prove his existence, except by doing something clearly God-like—something that is, humanly speaking, impossible?

But how can we be sure that these eyewitnesses didn't allow their fallibility to poke through as they described what they'd seen and heard? Maybe they misinterpreted events.

3. The writers were "carried" by the Holy Spirit as they wrote

Peter then says this:

> We also have the prophetic message as some-
> thing completely reliable, and you will do well to
> pay attention to it, as to a light shining in a dark
> place. *2 Peter 1 v 19*

He's speaking here of the Old Testament. It is, according to Peter, "completely reliable". For this reason:

> Above all, you must understand that no prophecy
> of Scripture came about by the prophet's own
> interpretation of things. For prophecy never had
> its origin in the human will, but prophets, though
> human, spoke from God as they were carried
> along by the Holy Spirit. *2 Peter 1 v 20-21*

Peter wants us to understand that the writers of Scripture (including himself[1]) weren't simply sharing their own expert opinions or experiences. When they wrote, they "spoke from God". When we read one of the 66 documents, we aren't reading "the prophet's own interpretation of things". Each author was "carried along" by God's Holy Spirit. In other words, the fallible, human authors weren't allowed to fall into error as they wrote. God's own Spirit would not allow it.

That's the reason for the 66 station single-minded-

---

1   Peter viewed his own testimony as having been guided and enabled by "the Holy Spirit sent from heaven." (1 Peter 1 v 12)

ness of Scripture; the single-mindedness of its origin. When we open it up and peer inside, we can see that it has one overarching storyline: the salvation of God's people. It has one purpose: to "make you wise for salvation through faith in Christ Jesus" (2 Timothy 3 v 15). It has one person as its main subject. And all of this is true because the Bible has one ultimate Author. "All Scripture," writes the Apostle Paul, "is God-breathed" (2 Timothy 3 v 16).

The single, divine author also explains something else you see in the Bible...

Fulfilled predictions

Scattered across the 66 documents, you'll see predictions and foreshadowings of future events. Roughly 2,500 of them. Of these, about 2,000 have already been fulfilled. More than 300 predictions refer specifically to Jesus, 29 of which were fulfilled in the final 24 hours of his life.

To give just two token examples. It's very hard to read Isaiah 53 (written more than 700 years before Jesus was born) and not see numerous foreshadowings of Jesus' life, death and resurrection.[1]

Or read Micah 5, written about 700 years before Jesus was born. There, you'll find a prediction that "one who will be ruler over Israel, whose origins are from of old"

---

1 You might expect a prediction of a future Messiah to be in the future tense. But you'll notice Isaiah 53 is in the past tense: "He *was* pierced...", rather than "He *will be* pierced..." You see this often in the Bible. The Holy-Spirit-inspired writers are so confident that God will do what he has promised, it's described as if it were already done.

will come from a little town called Bethlehem. The way this prediction comes to be fulfilled is described by Luke:

In those days Caesar Augustus issued a decree that a census should be taken of the entire Roman world. (This was the first census that took place while Quirinius was governor of Syria.) And everyone went to their own town to register.

So Joseph also went up from the town of Nazareth in Galilee to Judea, to Bethlehem the town of David, because he belonged to the house and line of David. He went there to register with Mary, who was pledged to be married to him and was expecting a child.   *Luke 2 v 1-5*

Mary is about to give birth to Jesus, and she's 80 miles away from Bethlehem, in Nazareth. Humanly speaking, it's hard to see how Micah's prediction of a Bethlehem birth can possibly be fulfilled.

But God governs everything, including governments. He sees to it that a census needs to be taken at precisely that time—one which requires each person to return to their home town. And Joseph's home town is... Bethlehem. The theologian John Piper writes:

Have you ever thought what an amazing thing it is that God ordained beforehand that the Messiah be born in Bethlehem (as the prophecy in Micah 5 shows); and that he so ordained things that when the time came, the Messiah's mother and legal father were living in Nazareth; and that in order

*to fulfill his word and bring two little people
to Bethlehem that first Christmas, God put it in
the heart of Caesar Augustus that all the Roman
world should be enrolled each in his own town?*

It's not just that the fulfilled prediction in itself is re-markable, although it is. Even more remarkable is God's absolute government of history, right down to the sub-sub-sub-atomic level of determining the decisions made in every human heart. As a result, Scripture is again proved true, even though from a human perspective, it would've seemed inevitable that Mary would have to give birth in Nazareth.

Are there any non-biblical documents which support biblical history?

There are. The Jewish historian Josephus, writing in about AD 93, includes two references to Jesus in his book *Antiquities of the Jews*.

The Roman historian and senator Tacitus also refers to Jesus and his early followers, who were "called Christians by the populace. Christus, from whom the name had its origin, suffered the extreme penalty during the reign of Tiberius at the hands of one of our procurators, Pontius Pilatus…"

There are other sources of interest too; for example, Pliny the Younger, Lucian of Samosata, Celsus, and the Dead Sea Scrolls.

Aren't some of the stories from Jesus' life just legends and later additions?

Author and pastor Tim Keller makes three observations on this point.

First of all, the Gospels were written **too early** to be legends. Many of the first readers were well able to remember the events which the Gospels claimed to report, so any fabrications would have been obvious. Paul, who wrote so much of the New Testament, was writing even earlier—about 15-20 years after Jesus' crucifixion. In Philippians 2, for example, he quotes an early Christian hymn that speaks of Jesus' divinity. So clearly, the idea of Jesus' remarkable power and authority wasn't something dreamt up long after the event by people trying to gain status for themselves.

Secondly, the Gospels are **too counterproductive** to be legends. If the early church wanted to fabricate stories about Jesus that would make them and their writing more credible, why include so many details that seem to undermine such an aim? For example, why have women as the first witnesses to the resurrection when the culture routinely rejected a woman's testimony as inadmissible in court? Why have Jesus in Gethsemane asking his Father if he might be spared the agony of the cross? Is that the sort of thing you'd expect from a fictional triumphant hero? And why make the Apostles appear so laughably slow to believe Jesus? Why make Peter, one of the most prominent leaders in the early church, appear so cowardly—unless it was what actually happened?

Thirdly, the gospels are **too detailed** to be legends. They're packed full of tiny, apparently innocuous pieces of information that make no sense unless explained as eyewitness details. Remember that the modern novel form wasn't around until about 300 years ago, so this level of detail in an ancient document would be completely unprecedented for a fictional story. The author C. S. Lewis was himself a professor of English Literature at both Oxford and Cambridge. He concluded: *"I have been reading poems, romances, vision literature, legends and myths all my life. I know what they are like. I know none of them are like this."*

Conclusion

Does the Bible seem to be God's word? Does it look like honey?

So far, the signs are promising. We've seen the extraordinary unity of Scripture, the credentials of the New Testament writers, and the remarkable way in which future events are predicted and fulfilled in its pages.

But is the Bible we hold in our hands today the same as the Bible when it was first written? That's the question we turn to now.

Chapter 4

Does the Bible seem to be God's word?

Canon, contradictions and criticisms

I f the Bible really is God's word, wouldn't it be reasonable to suppose that God would protect and preserve it, rather than allowing it to be lost or corrupted—as many other ancient documents have been?

In this chapter, we'll take a look at how we came to have the Bibles we have.

Who decided which books are in the Bible?

The documents that make up our Bibles are known as the "canon". Let's look at the Old Testament first.

The 39 books of the Old Testament were written between 1400 and 430 BC. Some of them, it seems, were recognised instantly by God's people as being "from God". Others may have taken a while longer to become part of Scripture. What is clear is that by the time of Jesus, there was strong agreement about which documents should be recognised as God's word—and it's a list that matches the Old Testament we have in our Bibles. As biblical scholar Robert Plummer puts it:

> *For Christians, accepting the thirty-nine book Old Testament canon is relatively easy. One might say, "Jesus and his Apostles affirmed the Jewish canon of the Hebrew Scriptures in their day. As a follower of Jesus, I affirm the same."*[1]

How do we know that the Old Testament in our Bibles is the same as the one Jesus refers to?

God commanded that his words be publicly preserved in the tabernacle—and later, in the temple—so that there would be no doubt about what God's words actually were. The Jewish historian Josephus tells us that the documents preserved in the temple (before its destruction in AD 70) were indeed the books that were recognized by the Jewish people as God's word, with divine authority. So we can be confident that our Old Testament lines up with the Scripture Jesus recognised as authoritative.

Tellingly, Jesus' religious opponents, though they were extremely keen to find fault with anything he said or did, never took issue with any of the Old Testament texts he quoted. So it's reasonable to assume that the books Jesus quoted had already been firmly established as God's word by the time of Jesus' ministry.

---

1   Robert L. Plummer, *40 Questions About Interpreting The Bible* (Grand Rapids: Kregel Publishing, 2010), page 58.

Having carefully analysed all the texts Jesus quotes, theologian John Frame concludes: "In my judgment, the data indicate clearly that this canon is identical with the canon endorsed by Protestants since the Reformation."[2]

What about the Apocrypha?

Some traditions (Roman Catholic and Eastern Orthodox, for example) include additional books in their Old Testament. Protestants don't consider these "apocryphal" books to be Scripture, for several reasons. For one thing, the Jewish authors who wrote the books never accepted them into their canon. They themselves put the books in a different category from the recognised Hebrew Scriptures.[3]

Who decided which books were included in the New Testament?

Sometimes people imagine that the contents of the New Testament were decided by a rabble of power-hungry factions with murky motives, each of which had a vested interest in certain books being—or not being—included.

In reality, the Bible is made up of books which were widely acknowledged as already having God's authority. The early church didn't wilfully "declare" certain books to be from God; they could only recognise what was already apparent.

In the case of the New Testament, the early church recognised only those books which were:

---

2   John Frame, *The Doctrine of the Word of God* (Phillipsburg: P&R Publishing, 2010), page 135.

3   For more on the Apocrypha, see Plummer, pages 63–65.

- ▓ **Apostolic.** Written by or closely connected to an Apostle (an authorised eyewitness of Jesus).

- ▓ **Widely embraced.** Already in common usage by the early church.

- ▓ **Orthodox.** Not contradicting any recognised apostolic book or teaching.

Having applied those three tests, the early church recognised as authoritative the 27 books we have in our New Testament. Irenaeus, who was born in about AD 130, was one of the so-called "Fathers" of the church. He wrote a book called *Against Heresies*, and in it he quoted as authoritative nearly every book of our present New Testament. The only ones he didn't quote from were Philemon, 2 Peter, 3 John and Jude. In other words, as early as the 2nd century, the churches widely regarded at least 23 of the 27 books in our New Testament as God's word. Taking into account the different backgrounds and theological leanings of the early Christians, their agreement about which documents belonged in the New Testament is remarkable. As one scholar writes: "It serves to suggest that this final decision did not originate solely at the human level".

By the way, this three-fold test of authenticity is the reason Christians don't recognise the authority of the so-called "alternative" Gospels which were written later, from the 2nd to the 4th century AD. All the documents in the New Testament canon can be dated prior to AD 100. It's also the reason why there will never be any new books added to the Bible. Even if an enterprising archaeologist turns up a previously unknown letter by the Apostle Paul, it would fall foul of the "widely used by the early church" test.

Why are the Old Testament books in the order they're in?

Although the books generally appear in historical order, there are some exceptions. That's because, in our English Bibles, the books are grouped primarily by topic rather than the order they were written in. Like this:

Law	History	Wisdom	Prophecy
Genesis	Joshua	Job	**"Major" Prophets**
Exodus	Judges	Psalms	Isaiah
Leviticus	Ruth	Proverbs	Jeremiah
Numbers	1-2 Samuel	Ecclesiastes	Lamentations
Deuteronomy	1-2 Kings	Song of	Ezekiel
	1-2 Chronicles	Solomon	Daniel
	Ezra		
	Nehemiah		**"Minor" Prophets**
	Esther		Hosea
			Joel
			Amos
			Obadiah
			Jonah
			Micah
			Nahum
			Habakkuk
			Zephaniah
			Haggai
			Zechariah
			Malachi

Why are the New Testament books in the order they're in?

As with the Old Testament, there's a logical flow to the order of books in the New Testament.

It begins with the "Gospels", four parallel histories of Jesus' life, death and resurrection. One of the Gospel writers, Luke, also provides a sequel (Acts), which records the "acts" of Jesus through the Apostles, as the early church gets started.

Then come the letters of the Apostle Paul, who wrote around half of the documents in the New Testament. The letters are included by decreasing order of size; first the letters he wrote to communities, then the ones he wrote to individuals. The anonymous letter to the Hebrews, intended for Jewish Christians, was apparently included next because it was believed to be from the pen of Paul, or at least from one of Paul's companions in ministry.

After that, there are the other New Testament letters. It's possible these letters appear in order of the authors' prominence in the early church.[1] Then comes the letter of Jude, the half-brother of Jesus.

And finally, there's Revelation. It doesn't fit neatly into the "letter" category. It's part letter, part prophecy and part apocalyptic literature. But it makes sense to place it last in the Bible: it looks forward to events yet to come; namely the return of Christ, the final judgement, and the creation of the new heaven and the new earth.

---

1   See the list of names Paul gives in Galatians 2 v 9.

Gospels and Acts	Letters by Paul	General letters and Revelation
Matthew	Romans	Hebrews
Mark	1-2 Corinthians	James
Luke	Galatians	1-2 Peter
John	Ephesians	1-3 John
Acts	Philippians	Jude
	Colossians	Revelation
	1-2 Thessalonians	
	1-2 Timothy	
	Titus	
	Philemon	

Why so many different versions of the Bible?

There's the NIV (New International Version). There's the ESV (English Standard Version). Then of course there's the KJV (King James Version). There's also the NLT, RSV and the NASB, to name but a few. Why so many?

These "versions" are different translations of the biblical documents into English. Translations are necessary because the original documents were written in Hebrew and "Koine" Greek, with a bit of Aramaic thrown in. Koine Greek (pronounced coin-ay) was a common form of Greek from the 4th century BC to the 5th century AD.

We might assume that one translation would be enough. But that's not the way translation works. Often, there isn't a single equivalent word in English. Things get even more challenging when you try to translate some of the "picture language"—metaphors and similes. So inevitably, the skill of the translator comes into play, and this results in different versions.

There is no "definitive" English translation of the Bible. Having said that, some are more accurate and readable than others (I'd suggest the NIV or ESV). Some are downright misleading and should be avoided at all costs (such as the *New World Translation*, which deliberately omits references to Christ's deity).

But the number of different translations needn't worry us. Just because there are 15 different English translations of Dante's *Divine Comedy*, it doesn't mean we can't know what Dante meant. However, it does mean that for serious students of the Bible, an awareness of the original languages is essential. If you're not great with languages, there are some terrific commentaries available, written by people who've spent years studying Hebrew, Greek and Aramaic.[1] They can be a great help in understanding the Bible better.

Doesn't the Bible have mistakes and contradictions in it?

If the original Bible documents had genuine contradictions and mistakes in them, then the claim to be God's word would be exposed as fraudulent, or at least ignorant. The Bible would no longer *seem to be* God's word. So this is an important question to ask.

One book, *When Critics Ask*, gives "answers to all the major questions ever asked about the Bible—over 800 in

---

1   For commentary recommendations, see D. A. Carson's *New Testament Commentary Survey* and Tremper Longman's *Old Testament Commentary Survey.*

all." Sadly, I'm not going to be able to take individual questions in turn. But let me suggest two reasons why we should pause before saying the Bible has mistakes in it.

First, we're finite. If the Bible really is God's word, we wouldn't expect our minds to grasp everything it says. We wouldn't always expect to be comfortable with it, or immediately agree with it. It would be strange if we did. There will be things that confuse us, confound us, shock us. Even for mature Christians, there will be places in the text where the most honest response is to admit our limits, and ask God to help us understand.

Secondly, we're sinful. Romans 1 tells us that sinful people actively "suppress the truth" of God. Christians should remember that although Jesus has liberated us from slavery to sin, we're not yet fully free of sin's effects. Our minds, even when we have the best of intentions, do not yet see as clearly as they will when we see Christ face to face. It may be that our perception of an "error" in the Bible says more about us than it does about the text. Theologian John Frame writes:

> When we deal with Bible problems, then, it is important for us to be aware of these limitations, that is, to read humbly. When we are faced with a problem, it is no dishonour to say, "I don't know how this can be resolved." Scientists do that all the time, when they encounter a phenomenon that seems to run contrary to a theory they believe. When the evidence for the theory is otherwise substantial, the scientist rightly assumes that the phenomenon can somehow be reconciled to

the theory, even if he doesn't know how that will happen.[1]

But there's another reason we should pause before saying the Bible has mistakes and contradictions in it. We may be misunderstanding what is meant when the Bible is said to be "without error".

What does "without error" mean?

Theologians call it "inerrancy". It's the idea that the Bible is completely truthful in everything it says.[2] Whether it speaks of geographical, historical or theological details, it is trustworthy.

However, the Bible's claim to be "without error" has some important, common-sense qualifications:[3]

1. It's not an error if it's not in the original documents

Especially where numbers are concerned, there are some errors in every Hebrew and Greek copy of the Bible. Unlike the writers of Scripture, the copyists weren't guided into "all truth" by the Holy Spirit (John 16 v 3).

Copy out the 40 chapters of Exodus, and chances are you'll have introduced one or two errors into the text. (Hopefully it wouldn't be a major blunder, like the

---

1   John Frame, *The Doctrine of the Word of God* (Phillipsburg: P&R Publishing, 2010), page 181.

2   To go deeper on this subject, see G. K. Beale, *The Erosion of Inerrancy in Evangelicalism.*

3   In this section, I'm leaning on the excellent work by Robert L. Plummer, *40 Questions About Interpreting The Bible*, 41-44.

1631 edition of the Bible which commanded its readers: "Thou shalt commit adultery".)

Some would claim that's reason enough not to trust the Bible. "You can't trust the Bible because it's like the game Telephone. One person whispers a sentence to someone else, who passes it to another, and by the time it gets to us, it's a completely different sentence. So no one really knows what was said originally."

However, although we no longer have access to the original biblical documents, all is not lost. The truly enormous number of surviving copies enables experts to reconstruct the original with great accuracy. This process of comparing copies is called textual criticism, and as a result, scholars are able to say: "*For over 99% of the words of the Bible*, we know what the original manuscript said."[4] The remaining less than 1% make no difference to any biblical doctrine or teaching.

Dan Wallace, a textual critic himself, has a good illustration of what this means. Imagine we have a 1,000-piece jigsaw puzzle. We don't have any pieces missing. Actually, we have many more pieces than are necessary to complete the puzzle. As a result, it's usually very obvious which are the extra ones that don't fit. In the same way, because we have so many surviving copies of the biblical documents, we have all we need to complete the "puzzle" of what the original documents said—and whatever is extra is obviously so.

As far as the New Testament goes, over 5,800 Greek

4   Wayne Grudem, *Systematic Theology* (Nottingham: InterVarsity Press, 1994), 96.

manuscripts and manuscript fragments have been cat-alogued. The total number (when you include early translations into other languages) hasn't yet been calcu-lated, but it numbers in the tens of thousands. As Dan Wallace explains: "We have more than 1,000 times the manuscript data for the New Testament than we do for the average Greco-Roman scholar."

2. It's not an error if we misunderstand the author's intention

When you open up a newspaper, you'll see many differ-ent kinds of writing.

Appearing alongside factual reports of world events, there may be celebrity gossip, infographics, stocks and shares, football league tables, book reviews, cartoons, and weather forecasts. Instinctively, most of us don't read a cartoon in the same way we read a war corre-spondent. In the same way, biblical authors write in a number of different "genres", and they expect us to read each one appropriately. If we read a war correspondent as if he were a cartoonist ("well this isn't funny *at all*"), the mistake will be ours rather than his.

In addition, biblical authors sometimes use meta-phors and similes that aren't intended to be taken liter-ally. This is why, when the newspaper's sporting corre-spondent informs us that a particular player is currently "on fire", we shouldn't become alarmed and call the fire brigade. It would be odd if we wrote an angry let-ter to the editor accusing the reporter of being in error because the player wasn't literally in flames.

It's also worth remembering that biblical writers were

using the literary conventions of their day. When, for example, Mark quotes two different Old Testament authors, introducing them with the phrase "As it is written in Isaiah…" (Mark 1 v 2), it's not because he got sloppy and forgot the second author. It's because Jewish writers sometimes cited only one spokesman when they combined several texts.

Likewise, it's not an error that the Gospel writers sometimes order their events differently. The authors make no claim to include all the events of Jesus' life, or to put those events in strict chronological order (see John 20 v 30-31). In fact, each writer wrote with a slightly different purpose in mind, and deliberately arranged the material to that end. Matthew, for example, wrote for a Jewish audience, so he emphasises the fulfilment of Old Testament prophecies. Mark, on the other hand, wrote for a non-Jewish audience, and deliberately leaves out many of those details.

3. It's not an error if it's a paraphrase

Sometimes a biblical writer will only report partially, paraphrase or summarise. If you asked a friend what they'd been up to last night, and they proceeded to give you an exact account of every single detail, complete with every single word they'd said to anyone, you wouldn't think they were being informative, you'd think they were being irritating. There's a level of detail that actually gets in the way, because you'd get so bored and confused you'd either walk off or glaze over. In the same way, when biblical writers summarise or paraphrase, they're not "making mistakes". They're telling the truth in a reasonable, digestible way.

4. It's not an error if it's "phenomenological language"

When humans describe things from their own vantage point rather than supplying an objective, scientific explanation, that's phenomenological language. An example would be when a TV weatherperson or a biblical author speak of "the sun rising". Nobody condemns a weatherman who says the sun will rise at 7am tomorrow morning. He's not making any claims about the earth being the centre of the universe. He's just describing things as they appear to be from our perspective. To be strictly scientifically accurate, he'd have to say: "Tomorrow at 7am, the earth will have rotated to such a degree that our particular region of the planet will be exposed to the sun's rays." And then, as well as being strictly scientifically accurate, he would also be unemployed.

5. It's not an error if someone else says it

The Bible often reports what people say. Not all of these people tell the truth, at least not all the time, and some of them make mistakes. In Psalm 14 v 1, we read: "There is no God." An obvious error in the Bible? No, it's the reported speech of someone who is in error: "The fool says in his heart, 'There is no God.'"

6. It's not an error if the Bible doesn't speak definitively or exhaustively on every subject

The Bible doesn't tell you how to put topspin on a tennis ball, win the Pulitzer Prize, or rustle up a jar of fresh plum chutney. Criticising the Bible for what it doesn't say is not the same as finding an error.

7. It's not an error if it ain't written proper

The biblical authors came from a wide variety of social and educational backgrounds. In the original languages, there are some sentences in Scripture which are, according to current standards, ungrammatical. As theologian Wayne Grudem says, these ungrammatical sentences are still without error "because they are completely true. The issue is *truthfulness* of speech."

Who's to say the Qu'ran isn't also God's word?

The Bible and the Qu'ran contradict each other at significant points.

For example, the Qu'ran (written in the 7th century) rejects the idea that Jesus was the Son of God, that he was ever crucified or resurrected, or that he ever atoned for the sins of his people. In fact, it goes even further, predicting that on the Day of Judgement, Jesus himself will deny he made any claim to divinity (*The Qu'ran*, 5th Surah, verse 116).

It's logically possible that the Qu'ran is God's word, or that the Bible is, or that neither are. But it's not logically possible for *both* of them to be the words of God. Either Jesus is the Son of God, or he isn't.

Aren't the stories about Jesus in the Bible just re-hashes of pre-biblical myths?

What would you say if I told you that the Egyptian god Horus was conceived by a virgin called "Meri"; that his birth was announced by angels and heralded by a star; had twelve disciples; raised people from the dead and walked on water; was crucified and resurrected? What if I suggested that the biblical portrait of "Jesus" is just a fictional mash-up of earlier gods?

Recently, this idea has become popular in some quarters. The only fly in the ointment, as scholars of ancient Egyptian mythology will explain, is that none of the above claims are true. Horus was conceived by a non-virgin called Isis, not "Meri"; his birth wasn't announced by an angel or heralded by a star; he had four disciples, not twelve; there's no reference to Horus raising the dead or walking on water; and there's no mention of him being crucified or resurrected.

But even if there were any similarities between Jesus and earlier, fictional gods, would it follow that Jesus is also fictional? Head on over to YouTube and you'll find a clip from the TV show *The Lone Gunmen* which features a story about slamming a fully loaded jet airliner into the World Trade Center. Remarkably, the show originally aired six months before September 11th, 2001. Does that mean 9/11 never happened?

Conclusion

In the first two chapters, we saw that the Bible claims to be from God. In chapters 3 and 4, we've looked inside and seen some remarkable features:

- The unity of the Bible. 66 documents, produced in wildly different circumstances, each developing an ongoing narrative about the same theme, and the same central figure.

- Fulfilled predictions.

- The eyewitness testimony of the New Testament. Every book written by (or under the guidance of) an Apostle. The rest written by eyewitnesses and companions of Jesus.

- The writers' insistence on the truth of what they'd written, even though it frequently resulted in persecution, torture and death.

- The fact that their writings, if false, could easily have been disproved. The extraordinary historical details they recorded could easily have been laughed out of circulation by talking to any one of the hundreds of eyewitnesses, most of whom were still alive when they "went to press". But their claims (outrageous though they were) stood up under enquiry.

- The remarkable agreement of the early church on which documents should be included. The Old Testament documents we have in a good modern translation of the Bible are the documents that were accepted as God's word in the time of Jesus. The New Testament documents we have are the same ones that were accepted as God's word by the early church.

■ The unparalleled number of surviving copies (and copy fragments) which enables us to construct the original text with tremendous accuracy.

In short, the Bible seems to be trustworthy. As we look inside, it seems to be what it claims to be.

But just because it says *honey* on the label, and it looks like honey on the inside...

There's nothing else for it. We need to taste.

Chapter 5

Does the Bible prove to be God's word?

Tasting, seeing, and the sweetness of Scripture

magine if I looked you in the eye and told you, "Your best friend doesn't exist".

You're a bit taken aback by this.

"What do you mean?"

"This 'friend' of yours? The one you're always talking about? I've never seen him."

"What—what are you saying?"

"I'm saying he's an *imaginary friend*. There's nothing wrong with that—I had one when I was small. But you're married with two children. Enough's enough."

You shake your head.

"But I've known him for years. He's absolutely real."

"Sorry," I say. "Don't believe you."

Now perhaps if we'd known each other for some time, I would give you the benefit of the doubt. And maybe if I knew that millions of other people also claimed to know this "friend", I wouldn't be quite so confrontational.

But that would only go so far. There comes a point where, if I'm to know *for certain* that this person exists, I must be introduced to him myself. There has to be a personal experience.

That's the stage we've reached with our question, "Can I really trust the Bible?" At this point, we need to take a final leaf out of Pooh's book. Having seen that the jar *claims to be* honey, and taken off the lid to see that the contents *seem to be* honey, we have to dip a finger inside and find out for certain. Does it *prove to be* God's word?

Taste and see

Our challenge comes, not from a children's storybook, but from the Old Testament itself. Psalm 34 says: "*Taste and see* that the LORD is good...".

Jesus says much the same thing in the New Testament:

> Anyone who chooses to do the will of God *will find out* whether my teaching comes from God or whether I speak on my own.
>
> *John 7 v 17*

Jesus is here speaking of what you will experience if you put his words into practice; you will find out for yourself whether his word can be trusted or not. In case they missed it, Jesus tells his disciples again: "Now that you know these things, you will be blessed *if you do them*"

(John 13 v 17). That's the deal: the blessing only comes when we act on what we read. We can only know for sure that it's honey when we are prepared to taste it for ourselves.

Shivering at the edge

When I was a little boy, I faced one of the biggest challenges of my life. The deep end of Banstead Swimming Pool. Shivering at the edge of the water, with my mother sitting on the wooden benches nearby, I peered down into 16 whole feet of frowning blue terror.

The swimming coach was a bluff Scottish man with an orange beard who'd presumably had enough of the Territorial Army and had decided to spend his Thursday evenings scaring children. "Right," he said, "in you go." As if it was the most normal thing in the world. What, just... jump in? "Yep, come on. Haven't got all day." My teeth chattered like a Gatling gun. "Nothing to be afraid of," he said, which seemed patently untrue.

But then two things happened. First, I noticed the swimmers already in the water. Whatever else they were doing, they weren't drowning. In fact, they seemed much happier than I was. Even children my own age were splashing each other and laughing riotously. As I reflected on this, it seemed reasonable to suppose that they knew something I didn't.

Secondly, I looked at the kind face of my mother. I knew that she loved me, would do nothing to harm me, and wanted me to be happy. As I looked over at her for reassurance, she mouthed the words: "It's ok". And then she smiled a wonderful "it's ok" smile.

But there was only one way to discover if that dark blue water would bear a fearful seven year-old. It wasn't enough to trust what others told me. I had to experience it for myself. Turn to Matthew 7, and you'll see the kind face of Jesus encouraging you to do the same. Three times, Jesus says that we must act on God's word for ourselves, if we're to know we can trust it:

> *Ask* and it will be given to you; *seek* and you will find; *knock* and the door will be opened to you. For everyone who asks receives; the one who seeks finds; and *to the one who knocks, the door will be opened*.
>
> *Matthew 7 v 7-8*

> Not everyone who says to me, "Lord, Lord," will enter the kingdom of heaven, but *only the one who does the will of my Father* who is in heaven.
>
> *Matthew 7 v 21*

> Therefore everyone who hears these words of mine *and puts them into practice* is like a wise man who built his house on the rock.
>
> *Matthew 7 v 24*

Jesus' challenge to you as you read the Bible is this: *do what it says*. Put it into practice. As you do that, and only as you do that, you'll find out for yourself that the Bible is what it claims to be, and what it seems to be.

But there's another reason for putting the Bible into practice. Jesus continues:

> ...everyone who hears these words of mine and *does not put them into practice* is like a foolish man who built his house on sand. The rain came down, the streams rose, and the winds blew and beat against that house, and it fell with a great crash.   *Matthew 7 v 26-27*

Nobody learns to swim simply by reading about it, talking about it, or hearing others talk about it. That wouldn't be much use if we were drowning. In the same way, Jesus is warning us that unless we act on his words by putting them into practice, they will leave us un-moved, unchanged, and unprepared for the judgment that is coming.

Beware of being Talkative

In John Bunyan's book *The Pilgrim's Progress*, we meet a cheery character called Talkative. There's nothing Talkative loves more than to talk about the glorious truths of the gospel: the Father's rightful anger averted, sins forgiven, guilt and shame removed, Christ's righteousness given to us, the inheritance of the new creation. He talks about the need for repentance and faith, the necessity of new birth, and the fact that our good works cannot save us. He knows how to refute false opinions, and instruct others. He has full assurance that he is heading for heaven.

But he is mistaken. Talking and doing are two different things, as James 1 v 22 makes very clear: "Do not merely listen to the word, and so deceive yourselves. *Do what it says.*" What makes Talkative so frightening is that he is absolutely convinced of his own salvation. Talkative has talked such a good talk for so long that he has managed to deceive himself. He has no idea that he is in terrible danger.

Jesus' warning, then, is intended for those who think they're Christian, at least as much as it's intended for those who know they're not. He's talking to the Talkatives of this world. I must ask you directly: have you ever been moved by an excellent sermon, an insightful Christian book, or a convicting conversation with a Christian friend—even to tears? Have you perhaps even commented about how very moving it was, and how very convicted you were—and then walked away from it and changed nothing? Jesus is speaking to you. If you do not actually *do* what the Bible tells you, you are being foolish, and you are in serious danger.

Yes, all Christians are dogged by besetting sins and deep-rooted idolatries, many of which we'll be battling until the day we see the Lord face to face. But what Matthew 7 makes graphically clear is that if we make a habit of hearing God's word without acting on it, we cannot presume on our safety.

The Author speaks

Sometimes, theologians speak about the "clarity" of Scripture. What they mean is that God has so written his word that it can be understood by ordinary believers. Psalm 119 v 130 puts it like this: "The unfolding of your words gives light; *it gives understanding to the simple*". As a result, real wisdom does not depend on how many college degrees we hold.

How is this possible? Through prayer, as we ask God to unfold his words to us. And also through the presence of God the Holy Spirit. Alive in every believer (see John 14 v 15-17), he is nothing less than the Author of Scripture, working in us so that we can understand the book he has written. And as we read, we receive from him an inward, experiential sense that confirms the truth of what we're reading. The Author speaks personally to us, saying silently, undeniably: "This is true".

Without the Holy Spirit within us we'll never trust the Bible. This is how the theologian John Calvin put it, writing in the 16th century:

> *...the testimony of the Spirit is more excellent than all reason. For as God alone is a fit witness of himself in his Word, so also* the Word will not find acceptance in men's hearts before it is sealed by the inward testimony of the Spirit. *The same Spirit, therefore, who has spoken through the mouths of the prophets must penetrate into our hearts to persuade us that they faithfully proclaimed what had been divinely commanded.*
>
> *By this power we are drawn and inflamed, knowingly and willingly, to obey him, yet also more vitally and more effectively than by mere human willing or knowing ... I speak of nothing other than what each believer experiences within himself.*

Try as I might to convince you, only the Holy Spirit himself can put the matter beyond doubt.

If God really wants to speak to us through the Bible, why is some of it so hard to understand?

I've recently been buried in Charles Dickens' classic novel *Bleak House*. It's not what you'd call beach reading. It's long, and sometimes I lose track of names and sub-plots. But if I said to you: "Yeah, I read that *Bleak House*. It's rubbish. Just a load of nonsense about lawyers and orphans. I gave up", it would be very revealing. Though you would be none the wiser about *Bleak House*, you would be very much the wiser about me.

Some books we read, but the best books read us. They assess us, make demands of us. They probe, they press. As a result, they're not always easy to read. The Bible is like that.

And that's a good thing. First, because hard texts have a way of humbling us. Hard texts remind us that the author is the triune God himself, whose wisdom infinitely outpaces our own. We shouldn't bristle when we discover that parts of the Bible exceed our current grasp.

Secondly, hard texts are good for us because God the Father wants us to become more like his Son. The only way this can happen is if our minds and hearts are exercised. The person who never wants the Bible to be hard is like the person who goes to the gym and never wants to sweat. If it never challenged or stretched us, it wouldn't have any power to make us change or grow. And incidentally, we shouldn't give up wrestling with the Bible just because it can be hard. If two Christians reach different conclusions about the same text, that doesn't mean we can never know what it actually means, or that we should give up trying to find out.

Bible-shaped

As people look for certainty that the Bible really is from God, they sometimes miss what seems—to me at least—to be very persuasive evidence.

The most Bible-shaped people I know are a wonder to me. You don't hear much about them in the media because their lives are self-sacrificial and other-centred. They love tirelessly and genuinely, in the background, under the radar. They want to find ways to encourage you or mourn with you or give you practical help. They are patient. They are kind. They take their Bibles seriously, but not themselves. They know how to laugh. Engage them in conversation, and they want to talk about you. They don't pelt their Facebook feeds with mock-humble pronouncements of their own greatness. And when others say that Christians are bigoted or stupid, they don't lose heart or respond with anger. They carry on, quietly loving and serving others.

The most Bible-shaped people I know have been men and women who opened their homes and their lives to me. They spent time with me. Loved me when I was at my least loveable. Some of them, having no education to speak of, spoke with a wisdom that left me slack-jawed. During periods of depression, when I was seemingly unreachable, they sat patiently with me, they put their arms around me. They never lost patience, they never lost hope. They called me to throw off the sin that so easily entangles, but they weren't shocked or self-righteous about any darkness they saw in me, because they acknowledged it in themselves. Love like that always protects, always trusts, always hopes, always perseveres. It isn't self-seeking, or easily angered, and it keeps no record of wrongs.

I've only ever seen love like that in two places. I've seen it in Jesus. And I've seen it in the most Bible-shaped people I know.

Don't read the Bible
Remember Psalm 19?

> The decrees of the Lord are firm,
>   and all of them are righteous.
> They are more precious than gold,
>   than much pure gold;
> they are sweeter than honey,
>   than honey from the honeycomb.
>
> *Psalm 19 v 9-10*

Later, another psalm returns to this theme, exclaiming: "How sweet are your words to my taste, *sweeter than honey to my mouth!*" (Psalm 119 v 103).

God's words aren't meant simply to be seen or heard. They are meant to be tasted. Things you only see or hear remain outside you. You can keep them at arm's length.

But you can't do that with things meant for tasting. You have to take them inside you. Into your mouth, onto your tongue, down into your stomach. They become a part of you. They change you.

That is the point of the Bible. It hasn't been given to us so that we can know *about* God. It has been given to us so that we can *know* God.

One of life's saddest ironies is that many who know their Bibles back to front do not know its Author. This is a grand and tragic exercise in missing the point, along the lines of someone who is thrown a flotation device and uses it to make a hat. A. W. Tozer was right:

> *The Bible is not an end in itself, but a means to bring men to an intimate and satisfying knowledge of God, that they may enter into Him, that they may delight in His Presence, may taste and know the inner sweetness of the very God Himself in the core and center of their hearts.*

The Bible, in other words, is for tasting. You've seen that the label says "Honey". You've looked inside and seen that it looks like honey. Now taste the sweetness. Proverbs 24 v 13 puts it like this: "Eat honey, my son, for it is good; honey from the comb is sweet to your taste. Know also that wisdom [from God's word] is like honey for you: if you find it, there is a future hope for you, and your hope will not be cut off."

Because God's word is as essential to humanity as food, Jesus was able to say: "Man shall not live on bread alone, but on every word that comes from the mouth of God" (Matthew 4 v 4). We wouldn't leave a delicious hot meal lying on the plate to go cold and rot; neither ought we to leave God's words lying on the page uneaten. Act on them. Take them deep inside you as if they were food, and allow them to nourish you, and change you, and enrich you. "It was God's word that made us," said the 19th-century preacher C. H. Spurgeon, "is it any wonder that his word should sustain us?"

What God is saying to each one of us now is what he said to the Old Testament prophet Ezekiel. In a vision, God commanded Ezekiel to "eat this scroll I am giving you and fill your stomach with it" (Ezekiel 3 v 3; see also Revelation 10 v 9-10). The scroll contained the words of God. Ezekiel does as he is commanded; and then comes this beautiful sentence: "So I ate it, and it tasted as sweet as honey in my mouth." Even when God's words are hard or challenging for us to obey—as they were for Ezekiel—they are always sweet, because they bring life and joy, quite beyond any other food the world has to offer.

Seeing the Son

About six months after my conversation with the young man in New Delhi, I began studying at Oxford. I hadn't been to church for years, at least not regularly, and had no desire to start. But then I found myself sidling into a wooden pew at St Ebbe's Church. I hadn't chosen to attend because of any theological or architectural leaning, but because the congregation counted among its number a particularly lovely second-year student of modern languages.

It was there, incidentally, that I met a man called

Tony Jones, who was the student worker at St Ebbe's. He invited me to meet him for coffee one afternoon in his study, though I didn't really see the point. Even after we'd met, I still wasn't sure I saw the point. Pretty much all we did was look at a short Bible passage together. Tony would throw out some questions to make sure I understood what I was reading, asked me how he could be praying for me, and that was about it. Then we'd doggedly repeat the process a week or so later. Poor man, I thought to myself. He's obviously lonely.

This continued throughout the winter, and into the spring. Tony challenged me to "taste" one of the four gospels for myself, which I did. And by the time Easter arrived, I knew when I sat down in Tony's overstuffed armchair that I wasn't doing it for his benefit. I had been introduced to Jesus Christ. I had known about him before, of course, but now—now, I knew him. The one through whom, and for whom, all things have been created. The one who had known me, and had set his loving kindness upon me before the universe had been spoken into being.

My life changed radically, and in the space of about a week. This wasn't apparent only to me, by the way. It was clear to the people around me, especially to those who knew me well. When I returned home during the Easter vacation, my mother knew I'd changed as soon as she saw me. "What's happened?" she smiled, as I walked through the front door. "You look... *different*."

I did. As I put God's word into practice, I was being filled with an exhilarating sense of purpose and joy. Damaged and damaging relationships were being healed. And above all, rather than the begrudging, dutiful knowledge that a Christian *ought* to obey Christ, I now had an irrepressible *longing* to obey him—whatever it might cost me in worldly terms. Because now that I knew him, I knew I could trust him.

Over the years, I began to realise that I was not the only one. With almost comic regularity, I met people whose lives had been changed for ever when, rather than offending Tony, they'd started meeting with him to read the Bible. And though, sadly, the relationship with the modern languages undergrad didn't work out, another relationship—infinitely satisfying and entirely unexpected—started to bloom in the place where she had been.

When you see the sun, you know it's bright. When you taste honey, you know it's sweet. When you see Jesus Christ in Scripture, you know he is Lord. And when you put God's word into practice, you know it's for real.

Conclusion

To help us grasp how powerful Scripture is, the biblical writers say it's like fire. To express how penetrating it is, they describe it as being sharper than any double-edged sword. To explain how vital it is for life, they speak of it as bread and milk, food and water. To show how necessary it is for seeing clearly, they speak of it as a light, and as a mirror. To communicate how much we need it if we're to be secure and grounded, it's spoken of as an anchor, and as a rock. To underline how valuable it is, they speak of it as being more precious than thousands of pieces of silver and gold. To convey the fact that it creates life, it's spoken of as being like a seed. And when it describes how satisfying it is, God's word describes itself as being sweeter than the very sweetest honey.

Taste and see.

uestions
Christians ask

Other titles in this series

How will the world end?

by Jeramie Rinne

Christians believe that history is moving towards a dramatic conclusion—that one day Jesus Christ will return in glory to judge the living and the dead. But there seem to be so many different views about how this will happen, and when it will take place. How can we make sense of it all? This short, readable book explains clearly and simply the liberating reality of what the Bible is actually saying about the return of Christ and the end of the world.

Why did Jesus have to die?

by Marcus Nodder

Our culture ignores it. Many within the church seem to be almost embarrassed by it. Many others understand that the cross of Christ is at the very heart of Christian faith and life. This short, readable book explains clearly and simply what the Bible, and Jesus himself, say about the cross, and how Christians should understand it today.

Order from your local Good Book website:
UK & Europe: www.thegoodbook.co.uk
North America: www.thegoodbook.com
Australia: www.thegoodbook.com.au
New Zealand: www.thegoodbook.co.nz

Questions
Christians ask

Other titles in this series

Did the devil make me do it?
by Mike McKinley

When Jesus walked the earth, he cast out demons and had powerful encounters with the devil. But who exactly is the devil, and where did he come from? And what is he up to in the world today? This short, readable book explains clearly and simply what we can say with certainty from the Bible about Satan, demons and evil spirits.

Who on earth is the Holy Spirit?
by Tim Chester and Christopher de la Hoyde

Many people find it easy to understand about God and Jesus, but struggle to understand quite how and where the Holy Spirit fits into the picture. Who exactly is he? And how does he work in our lives? This short, simple books are designed to help Christians understand what God has said in the Bible about these questions and many more.

Order from your local Good Book website:
UK & Europe: www.thegoodbook.co.uk
North America: www.thegoodbook.com
Australia: www.thegoodbook.com.au
New Zealand: www.thegoodbook.co.nz

thegoodbook
COMPANY